Happy 1st Birthday Braden!

Love From, Uncle Steve & Aunt Danielle

XOXO XOXO

Happy 1st Birthday Braden!

Love From, Uncle Steve & Aunt Danielle

XOXO XOXO

Ode to Newfoundland

GEOFF BUTLER

LYRICS BY SIR CAVENDISH BOYLE

Tundra Books

Published in Canada by Tundra Books,
481 University Avenue, Toronto, Ontario M5G 2E9

Published in the United States by Tundra Books of Northern New York,
P.O. Box 1030, Plattsburgh, New York 12901

Library of Congress Control Number: 2002112851

National Library of Canada Cataloguing in Publication

Butler, Geoff, 1945-
   Ode to Newfoundland / Geoff Butler.

ISBN 0-88776-631-5

   1. Newfoundland and Labrador--Miscellanea--Juvenile literature.
2. Newfoundland and Labrador--Songs and music. I. Title.

FC2161.2.B88 2003	j971.8	C2002-904643-2
F1122.4.B88 2003		

We acknowledge the support of the Canada Council for the Arts and the Ontario Arts Council for our publishing program.

We acknowledge the financial support of the Government of Canada through the Book Publishing Industry Development Program (BPIDP) for our publishing activities.

The words and music to "Ode to Newfoundland," as they appear in this book, comprise the provincial anthem of Newfoundland and Labrador, in accordance with The Provincial Anthem Act.

Design by Cindy Elisabeth Reichle

Printed and bound in Hong Kong, China

1 2 3 4 5 6   08 07 06 05 04 03

To the people of
Newfoundland and Labrador

When the sun rises over North America, the first land to see the break of day is Newfoundland. On Newfoundland's northeast coast, perhaps people can even get an advance peek at the rising sun by looking over land's edge, beyond the place the Flat Earth Society calls one of the four corners of the earth. Maybe "living on the edge" accounts for the rich and vibrant culture of Newfoundland.

The centuries-old relationship that inhabitants of Newfoundland have with the sea has created a strong sense of place. The language of the provincial anthem, "Ode to Newfoundland," reflects that connection by expressing the natural beauty of Canada's easternmost and newest province.

Anthems often refer to victories or exploding bombs to arouse patriotic feelings. "Ode to Newfoundland" is noteworthy because it refers instead to glorious sun rays and a land that is windswept and even frozen. There is a verse for each season. Here people are expected to live with nature, and how they do this says a lot about their character.

Sir Cavendish Boyle, governor of Newfoundland from 1901 to 1904, wrote the words to "Ode to Newfoundland." The music was later composed by Sir C. Hubert H. Parry and officially approved as the music for the anthem in May 1904. This was long before Newfoundland joined Confederation. Today "Ode to Newfoundland" is the anthem for the Province of Newfoundland and Labrador.

The paintings I've created to accompany the lyrics are based largely on my memories of growing up in Newfoundland. As you turn the pages, you'll notice the words to the anthem on the left-hand side, displayed on parchment and held by two puffins. The birds encourage the chorus below to sing from the bottom of their hearts to the tops of their lungs, as they bob up and down on the water. On the right-hand side, the images follow the words by showing activities from the four seasons.

As the people of Newfoundland and Labrador face new challenges in the seasons ahead, they might be heard humming or singing this old song that they refer to simply as "The Ode." May it be as enduring as The Rock they call home.

GEOFF BUTLER

When sun rays crown thy pine-clad hills
And Summer spreads her hand,

6

When silvern voices tune thy rills,
We love thee, smiling land.

We love thee, we love thee,
We love thee, smiling land.

When spreads thy cloak of shimmering white
At Winter's stern command,

Through shortened day and starlight night,
We love thee, frozen land.

We love thee, we love thee,
We love thee, frozen land.

When blinding storm gusts fret thy shore,
And wild waves lash thy strand;

Though spindrift swirl and tempest roar
We love thee, wind-swept land.

We love thee, we love thee,
We love thee wind-swept land.

As loved our fathers, so we love,
Where once they stood we stand;

Their prayer we raise to Heaven above,
God guard thee, Newfoundland.

God guard thee, God guard thee,
God guard thee, Newfoundland.

28

The Atlantic Puffin (throughout)

The Atlantic puffin is one of the emblems of Newfoundland and Labrador. When it is laden down with small fish in its sea-parrot beak, skipping along the water and trying to get airborne, it almost looks like this symbolic Newfoundlander is trying to keep from falling over the edge of a flat earth. But puffins, like Newfoundlanders, are quite at home on the water. In fact, Newfoundland culture has developed because of the sea's bounty. No doubt the people of the province, noted for their humor, feel well-done by to be represented by a funny-looking seabird.

Western Brook Pond (page 7)

You will find Western Brook Pond on Newfoundland's west coast in Gros Morne National Park, a UNESCO World Heritage Site with a unique and spectacular geological landscape. It must have been someone with a wry sense of humor who called such a majestic fjord a pond, because ponds aren't generally walled in by cliffs measuring over half a kilometer, or two thousand feet high.

Perhaps it was Sir Cavendish Boyle's sense of humor that caused him to pen the words "pine-clad hills." This is not an image of Newfoundland that springs readily to mind now, though possibly it did when he was governor of Newfoundland.

The Newfie Bullet (page 9)

The train that traversed Newfoundland from the late 1890s to the late 1960s was known as the Newfie Bullet because it ran so slowly. A joke was that the Newfie Bullet was mentioned in the Bible because "the Lord makes everything that creeps and crawls."

Berry Picking (page 9)

Picking berries on the marshes or barrens has always been a good reason for an outing. A favorite fruit of New-foundlanders is an amber-colored berry called the bakeapple (also known as the cloudberry, *Rubus chamaemorus*). Another popular berry is the blueberry. A story is told of a visitor to Newfoundland who saw blue-berries in their unripe state and asked, "What are those red berries on the bushes over there?" When told they were blueberries, he said, "But they're red." *Oh yes, Sir*, the Newfoundlander replied, *the blueberries are red because they're green.*

The Capelin Scull (page 9)

In this painting a man is using a cast-net to catch capelin, small smeltlike fish. It seems that most everything in the sea, including cod, likes to eat capelin.

The migration of capelin from deep sea to inshore waters is called the capelin scull. It is a sight to behold, for during June and July, capelin spawn in the millions upon the beaches. When the call is heard, "The capelin are in," people run with nets and buckets to catch them. Capelin are used for food, bait, or garden fertilizer.

Codfish (page 11)

Traditionally, in Newfoundland, fish means codfish. In days gone by, the cod could be quite large – as large, perhaps, as the person who caught them. When the Europeans first arrived in Newfoundland waters, it's said (if fishermen are to be believed) they had trouble rowing their small boats because the fish were so plentiful. Nowadays, it's easy rowing.

Jigging (page 11)

Jigging means fishing with a weighted, unbaited hook attached to a line and jerked sharply upwards. Jigging for squid (to be used for bait) gave rise to one of Newfoundland's most popular of songs: "The Squid-Jiggin' Ground."

The Newfoundland Dog (page 13)

The Newfoundland is so well known there is really no need to add the word *dog*. It is, by nature, a water dog and has big webbed feet to prove it. Its feats of rescuing people from the water are legendary. While the Newfoundland is very much a working dog used for such things as pulling carts, carrying loads, and rescuing people, it is also a great companion.

The Newfoundland Pony (page 13)

The Newfoundland pony is small and tough and was once nearly extinct. Like the Newfoundland dog, and indeed Newfoundlanders themselves, it descends from hardy European forebears.

The Mummers (page 15)

The Christmas season is a time for visiting. One particular group of visitors is the mummers, or jannies. Mummers dress up in outrageous outfits, knock on doors, and – disguising their voices – ask, "Any mummers allowed in?" Once inside, they dance and sing and generally act the fool, until the host identifies them. After some refreshments, they are on their way to the next house.

Mummering goes on for the twelve days of Christmas. It starts on December 26 – St. Stephen's Day, or Boxing Day, as it's now called – and ends on Old Christmas Day, January 6, also known as Epiphany. William Shakespeare named his play *Twelfth Night*, after this festive time of year.

A Time (page 17)

A Newfoundland time is a party at a communal gathering, such as a church social or fundraiser. It starts with a sale of work, or craft sale. There are games and fun activities such as grab bag or fishpond, in which you grab or fish for small prizes. Afterward, there is a meal and, because the whole community comes out, there are several sittings – called first table, second table, and so on – until everybody gets fed. Then the tables are pushed aside, and the dance begins. In days past, the entertainer was called a fiddler regardless of what musical instrument he played, whether it was an accordion or a comb and tissue paper.

L'Anse aux Meadows (page 19)
At L'Anse aux Meadows, on the tip of the Great Northern Peninsula, there is a replica of a Viking settlement. It is a National Historic Site and a UNESCO World Heritage Site. Five hundred years before Columbus set sail, the Norse had already made the first European contact with North America. It is with some irony that the name L'Anse aux Meadows, the site where these hardened adventurers landed, may be a corruption of the French L'Anse aux Méduses: the cove of jellyfish.

The Beothuk (page 19)
Among the indigenous cultures of Newfoundland was that of the Beothuk people. Their culture came to a brutal end in the early 1800s, the result of a tragic clash of cultures. In this painting, the splayed ribs of an old boat, the *Beothuk*, represent this very sad chapter in the history of Newfoundland.

Tuckamores (page 19)
Tuckamores are small evergreen trees that are stunted because of pelting winds and salt spray. Some might not be much more than knee high and are so tough and gnarled you could almost dance a jig on the flattened tops.

Brimstone Head, Fogo Island (page 21)
Perhaps, with only the great expanse of the Atlantic on either side, the Flat Earth Society felt that Brimstone Head on Fogo Island was one of the four corners of the earth. I prefer to think it felt that the islanders would get a kick out of being told they lived at the end of the world.

Guy Fawkes Night (page 23)
On November 5, Newfoundlanders observe Guy Fawkes Night. This was the date in 1605 when Guy Fawkes attempted to burn the Parliament buildings in England. Today, the celebration is more of an excuse to build bonfires. It is a fun, lighthearted time indeed.

The Caribou (page 23)
During World War I, on July 1, 1916, the Newfoundland Regiment was practically wiped out at Beaumont-Hamel in France during the Battle of the Somme. Later on in the war, the Regiment was awarded the designation *Royal* in honor of its heroic sacrifices. While July 1 is now a jubilant Canada Day, part of the day is still treated with solemnity and remembrance in Newfoundland. The caribou, native to Newfoundland, is on the insignia of the Royal Newfoundland Regiment. A caribou monument overlooks that tragic battlefield in France where Newfoundlanders fell in such numbers. It is said to be looking toward Newfoundland.

Resettlement (page 25)
During the resettlement program of the 1950s and '60s, the government of Newfoundland and Labrador closed down small outports and moved people to so-called growth centers, where living conditions were expected to be better for all. Fogo Island, where I was born, was one place slated for resettlement. The people there resisted, and the film documentary technique that was used to form alternative policies has come to be known as The Fogo Process. The Fogo Process is now used in developing countries to foster community awareness.

Iceberg Alley (page 25)
It is not uncommon, even in summer, to see icebergs in Iceberg Alley. Iceberg Alley is that long route that icebergs take as they drift southward in the Labrador current toward the Gulf Stream. In my parents' time, people boated out to them to get some ice for ice cream. They were careful not to get too close to the icebergs, though, because there was always the danger of their floundering. Nowadays visitors can taste ice chipped off from "bergy bits" or "growlers" (smaller pieces of ice named for the noises they make as they float on the water). It's not everywhere or everyday that you can get samples of fresh water that are over ten thousand years old.

Fish Stages (page 27)
Fish stages are elevated structures at the water's edge where fishermen land and process fish. Because of the rocks and steep slopes they are built upon, it is necessary to use stilts as supports. All this may look precarious, but think of this homespun bit of engineering as Newfoundland's early entry into the world of high-rises.

Copying (page 27)
The dangerous activity called copying – jumping from one ice pan to another – probably developed from a game of follow the leader on frozen harbors. It is also a skill required by sealers in confronting the hazards of hunting on ice floes.

The Rock (page 29)
Newfoundland became Canada's newest province on March 31, 1949, barely missing out on becoming so on April Fool's Day. While the referendum vote on this issue was close, most Newfoundlanders today feel it would have been foolish not to have joined Canada. Both "Ode to Newfoundland" and "O Canada" are sung with affection at public functions.

Newfoundland is referred to fondly as The Rock. Anyone who's ever tried to dig a hole in Newfoundland soil will understand why. But this is not just any old rock. The friendliness of the Newfoundland people shows that, at its core, The Rock has a heart of gold.

1.

When sun rays crown thy pine-clad hills
And Summer spreads her hand,
When silvern voices tune thy rills,
We love thee, smiling land.

Refrain

We love thee, we love thee,
We love thee, smiling land.

2.

When spreads thy cloak of shimmering white
At Winter's stern command,
Through shortened day and starlight night,
We love thee, frozen land.

Refrain

We love thee, we love thee,
We love thee, frozen land.

3.

When blinding storm gusts fret thy shore,
And wild waves lash thy strand;
Though spindrift swirl and tempest roar
We love thee, wind-swept land.

Refrain

We love thee, we love thee,
We love thee wind-swept land.

4.

As loved our fathers, so we love;
Where once they stood we stand;
Their prayer we raise to Heaven above,
God guard thee, Newfoundland.

Refrain

God guard thee, God guard thee,
God guard thee, Newfoundland.